I SEE YOU EVERYWHERE!

42 No-fluff Principles to Stand Out and Sell More

*"Proven Methods to Build Influence,
Connect with People and
Multiply Your Brand's Footprint"*

© Paul Edwards, Jason Todd

ISBN 979-8-9905562-0-1

Emissary

Published in Phoenix, Arizona by Emissary Publishing.
Emissary is a business trade name of Ed's Voices, LLC.

Scan for more stand-out ideas!

Emissary Weekly Digest

- ✗ Fluff
- ✅ Marketing tips
- ✅ Book recommendations
- ✅ Podcast recommendations
- ✅ ... and even more goodness!

Table of Contents

Introduction

In separate careers and lives, we both heard the phrase "I see you everywhere!" from people we knew.

We took it seriously because it was accurate. It was one of the most evident signs our strategies worked, foreshadowing what we do today.

Together, we assist and facilitate founders and entrepreneurs in the most challenging part of growing a business and multiplying influence: informing the marketplace that you exist and persuading them why they should care.

If you start by simply showing up consistently as your authentic self, embodying your brand message and experience ... you can nurture a groundswell–a network of peers and affiliates who recommend and endorse you as a brand.

When your peers say, "I see you everywhere!" It's a sign that your reputation precedes you. It means the perceptions and opinions of your peers reach the eyes and ears of your audience (on your behalf) *before* the audience is in your physical proximity.

If you channel time, energy, and resources into building on that groundswell ... you can scale what you accomplish organically. You can begin to matter to people ... before you meet them.

The essence of great products and messages is when trust transfers from one human being to another. This book teaches you how to build the first level of confidence without spending enormous amounts of money or wasting tons of energy.

Chapter One
Magnetism

I (Paul) am not a science guy. But I enjoy how often the world of physics, chemistry, and biology make plain the invisible, spiritual world. Magnetism is a great example.

Magnetism requires *opposites* - positive and negative. When I first heard this, I winced a little. Attracting "opposites" sounded like a bad idea, like a single lady who keeps attracting bad dates. Who wants to be full of positive energy and only attract negative energy?

I think that would be true IF magnets attracted sludge ... but they don't. They attract *similar* substances. Don't take it to mean you, as a positive person, must attract negative people into your orbit. You want to attract *like-minded* people of similar substance who are <u>different</u> from you. By "different," I mean they are deficient where you're abundant, and vice versa.

Magnets also *repel*. Take two magnets, try pushing them together, and see what happens. Only by flipping one of the magnets, matching positive to negative, do they go "zap" and attach. It's no good trying to build magnetism in rooms full of clones of yourself (if such rooms existed). There must be positives that match your negatives and negatives that your positives can match.

You might think, "Well, that's true of any room you walk into. Everybody is strong at one thing and weak at another." Depending on your objective, you might be right—it may matter very little. It might not be as important if your business is universal, such as payment processing, accounting, or ISP. But experience suggests otherwise. I've known many "universal" business owners frustrated by networking. If you have 500 competitors nearby, it's hard to stand out.

During my insurance days, I frequently rubbed elbows with a guy who was my go-to advisor for Comcast. At the time, Comcast faced no severe competitors in our area; for the internet, it was "Comcast or bust." That made my friend the "only guy in town" - or at least, the only guy I knew who bothered to show up. So, there's an example of how you can quickly become magnetic. If you work in a "blue ocean" environment with no competitors ... who else will people turn to?

As for me, I worked in a "red ocean" industry. Property/casualty insurance was, by 2013, so commoditized and trivialized that the battle boiled down to who had the funniest commercials. GEICO, Progressive, State Farm, and Farmers Insurance were all known for their gag ads. In particular, GEICO sloganeered the expression "Fifteen minutes could save you fifteen percent or more on car insurance" into the American psyche. So, before too long, I stopped wasting time by appealing to an average consumer household and turned to serving business owners.

Entrepreneurs are a different breed. Their mentality blends well with my philosophy of personal responsibility, extreme ownership, and understanding context.

Being magnetic with business owners proved worthwhile and profitable. I joined the local chapter of the Multiple Listings Sales Association (MLSA), where 60-75 people met weekly in a local restaurant. Most people in the room were real estate agents, mortgage lenders, and "affiliates" - businesses from pest control to plumbing to home inspectors - who owned and operated their shops.

An opportunity arose to speak. I'd avoided volunteering to talk because I wasn't sure what to say, but controversy arose after Congress passed the 2012 Flood Insurance Reform Act. Suddenly, several agents and brokers had real estate deals in nearby flood zones jeopardized by national legislation. As the only insurance agent in the group who paid attention to the story, I spotted the link immediately and volunteered to give a short presentation.

Bingo. I'd struck my first "well" of magnetism.

Most of the agents and lenders who approached me after my presentation to thank me were caught off-guard by the news. I'd alerted an entire room of people to avoid doing deals in flood zones. My first client from MLSA, a lady from a local title insurance company, walked up and said, "Thanks for sounding the alarm! I'd like to have you look over my insurance, and maybe we'll see what you can come up with."

So remember to find a way to create "pull" with like-minded people. Educate and inform them where they're vulnerable while showing respect for their expertise. Give value upfront, without any thought of return, and you will draw people toward you. Be a magnet, not a "pusher." Magnets never have to push anything.

Reverse Magnetism

The other thing to remember about magnetism is the concept of *magnetic reversal*. Put simply, it's where one pole of a magnetic spectrum "trades" places with its opposite.

Insurance salesmen get caricatured for a reason - they usually appear pushy, desperate, and conniving. I tried hard-selling people for a short time, and it failed miserably. I stink at being "direct, in a charming way."

A few years later, one of my clients invited me to a mixed martial arts competition. It was a primarily blind invitation. Almost everyone there was a stranger. My client introduced me to his friends as "my insurance guy." I shook hands and greeted people ... *but never spoke about insurance.*

You might think this was a little extreme or applicable only when you sell a commoditized and caricatured product like insurance. But I'd learned to engage in magnetic reversal when people mentioned my occupation. If you want to talk about whatever you sell, sometimes the best way to get people to talk about it is to NOT talk about it.

Why does this work? Most people *expect* you to talk about your product or service. They *expect* to be prospected or approached as a number. The last thing they expect is that you will be unconcerned about your bottom line and treat them like regular people. It piques our curiosity when encountering someone who doesn't fit the template.

After a while, a conversation broke out among the group. A few of my client's friends began to rib me about my occupation to see how I handled their jokes. They asked a mixture of serious and humorous questions, which led to an unforgettable moment: pretending to be upset, tongue-in-cheek like a dissatisfied consumer getting an after-hours call from a boiler room salesman, I exclaimed: "I didn't come here to talk about insurance! I want to watch the competition! Leave me alone!"

The whole group fell out laughing, including me.

Magnetism depends on your ability to match positives to negatives, as we've covered. If you approach indirectly, with a patient, unhurried, relaxed, and relatable demeanor ... you show up as the positive - and "pull" the right people into your orbit.

A word of caution: the "right" people may not be who you expect them to be. Sometimes, they're the "right people in training." Remember the law of averages - fewer than 5 percent of people you meet are ready to buy on the spot. The same goes for people who will *never* buy from you - 20% of the total. That leaves 75% of everyone you meet on a "spectrum" of readiness to purchase from you. You should expect:

- To get along and be able to build relationships with 3 out of 4 people
- To be cordial and polite, but expect absolutely nothing from 1 out of 5 people
- To receive immediate orders or interest from 5 out of 100 people

These numbers shift as you get "smarter" about where you direct your energy. You become more familiar with your avatar client and how to find them, and you spend less time spinning your wheels or needing to go through 100 people to find five who will buy.

Just remember - most people who respond positively to you need a real-life "nurture sequence" of interaction before they buy. So, <u>never</u> be in a rush unless they are.

Now ... be magnetic. In the next chapter, we'll discuss curating your target audience.

Chapter Two
The Curated Audience

When you think of great communicators, who comes to mind? One of my (Jason) favorite speakers is leadership expert John Maxwell, who said:

> *"Educators take something simple and make it complicated, while communicators take something complicated and make it simple."*

If you believe you have a product, service, or message that will change the world, you must become skilled at communicating it. That means you need to be able to cut through the noise, reach a target recipient where they are, and quickly offer them a valuable message that's likely to trigger a response.

It sounds simple ... but then you have to do it. In my experience, most people get thrown off-track by ignoring a cardinal rule of marketing: **know your audience**.

To "know" your audience means defining, understanding, and speaking directly to them—entrepreneurs who do this experience the most significant momentum and success in the marketplace.

I've advised many entrepreneurs who have wasted time, money, and energy trying a "shotgun" approach to communication. In the worst cases, they flailed about, sending unwanted emails and spam messages on social media to strangers who could care less. The business owners refused to spend a second researching the target audience they wanted to reach and even less time surveying or analyzing feedback and data.

That's the wrong way to go about it! People avoid market research because they think it's tedious and difficult. They imagine hiring expensive agencies, spending months conducting focus groups, making endless phone calls, or bugging people during dinner for responses. That may be how they did it in the past ... but today is different.

When Paul and I launched Emissary Publishing, he said, "I know people pay for our service, but I don't run into them all the time. How can we be confident people truly want this?"

It was the right question to ask, and during that conversation, we set about answering some of the key questions we needed to answer through our market research. For your brand to become "contagious," it must have a firm grasp of what its intended audience wants. Run your message through the following list of questions:

Can you identify the product or service?

You must have a minimum viable product people will take seriously. They exchange money for products and services when they have confidence those products and services will solve their problems. So, if you have something to offer the market, be sure it has a name that tells the buyer what problem it will solve for them.

A friend of mine launched a skin care product aimed at middle-aged husbands and fathers, but he struggled with what to name it, especially since he lacked an established label like Calvin Klein or Davidoff. We settled on the name *Guardian*, which neatly described the family man, protecting and providing for his wife and children. Simultaneously, it implied "guarding" the man's skin against dryness and cracking.

Who already offers what you want to sell?

Most of the time, successful products offer a different angle on something that already exists. Chances are, your product or service is not a "unicorn" or a breakthrough innovation. So, you need to research and find out how competitors are positioned and differentiate yourself from them.

Of course, the most potent distinction you can make is usually the *experience* of working with you or using your product. But since your target market doesn't know that, it'll take time to consider how you distinguish yourself. What you should *not* do, however, is try to imitate competitors' brands. This only serves to create confusion in the minds of your potential customers.

Who is the buyer persona?

If you were face-to-face with your potential buyer, would you know? What characteristics would they have? Are they male or female? Are they single or married with children? Do they live in a particular geographic area? What kind of income do they earn?

A radio station we know of spent years studying their target listener, a 35-year-old wife and mother they named "Jess." They called her that based on the popularity of the name around the time she was born, and they kept a detailed spreadsheet of everything they knew about her. They knew her aspirations, what she dreamed about, and where she spent most of her time. They curated their playlist to create an "ambiance" soundtrack that followed her wherever she went.

Could you cite details like this about your target audience? If so, what would they be?

Surveys and Interviews

There's nothing like the ease of giving a person something you already know they want. When I (Paul) grew up, my parents' style of Christmas shopping focused on thoughtful gifts we would "guess" the other person wanted. I got quite a few gifts I didn't ask for and very little of what I wanted! We probably could have "surveyed" each other to see what we wanted … but it never occurred to us.

When we started Emissary, Jason counseled me to conduct some informal surveys. I bristled at first because I thought he meant using tools like SurveyMonkey and creating lengthy questionnaires. I did not look forward to it.

Instead, he told me to send a quick message to people I already knew on LinkedIn and ask if they'd be willing to hear a one-minute summary of our offerings. I messaged over 50 people in my network who fit or resembled the profile of our target audience, and almost all of them responded with eagerness to help.

Analyze the Data

When the people responded, I sent them 60-second audio messages describing three details:

- The main "problem" or "gap" in the market
- The solution we offered
- The price point we thought was reasonable

I added: "My questions are, 'Do you think we understand the problem?' 'Do you think we offer a good solution?' And 'does that price point scare you?'" I kept a spreadsheet of their answers. Of the 45 people who responded, I got 38 positive responses.

Of course, market research can become much more detailed and sophisticated. But for our purposes, we only wanted to know whether there was a good chance people would seriously consider our offers. A month or so later, we published our first title.

Champions, Supporters, Resistors and Bystanders

Audiences should include **champions**, **supporters**, **resistors,** and **bystanders**. It's your job to remember that you need all four and work hard to include them in any surveying and analysis you undertake.

My (Jason) mom has always been my biggest fan, as most mothers are. When I exhibited talents in music, computer programming, and entrepreneurship, she lavished praise and encouragement on me. Which was excellent, I suppose ... but there were times when I'd have preferred constructive criticism—usually whenever I failed.

Most moms are **champions**. They're unflappably committed to your success and adore everything about you. Champions are great people in your corner ... but champions tend to overlook or ignore your vulnerabilities and blind spots. They think so highly of you that they have trouble acknowledging your faults and failures.

That is why you need **supporters**—people who are just as excited about you but bring greater objectivity when evaluating your work. Supporters usually have experience or authority in the field you want to play in. They can sense when you're playing to your strengths and when you need help. Coaches, consultants, and mentors usually fit into this category.

The real test of your product or service lies in the responses of **resistors** and **bystanders**. They are crucial because they represent the entire planet of human beings—a population group much larger and more potent than your close circle of champions and supporters. If you launch a small product your friends and family can afford, they will buy it whether or not they need it, just to support you. But resistors and bystanders? That's a tougher nut to crack.

Resistors and bystanders form the great mass of the niche you wish to serve, even if it's only a few thousand people. That's a *lot* of people who don't know you! Why should they care? What's in it for them? How are they supposed to decide, in seconds, whether to pay attention to what you offer?

With resistors and bystanders, you must demonstrate respect for two cold, complex realities: (a) they don't know you personally or know much about what you offer, and (b) they have dozens of details competing for their attention and focus.

Hopefully, this chapter has helped you see how much thought and energy goes into properly curating an audience. In the next chapter, we'll cover building a solid brand that reflects your values.

Chapter Three
Building Your Brand

I (Paul) like startups that make private jet travel affordable for the average business owner. The idea of driving to the airport, parking in a small lot (where there's always plenty of space), walking 20 feet into a private terminal, avoiding security lines, and flying a small aircraft with maybe 5-7 other passengers is irresistible. It's consistent with how I live; I just want to *take action* rather than go through an airport dog-and-pony show.

These companies easily attract my attention with their advertising on social media. I look at almost every ad and imagine myself aboard one of their jets. Their messaging works because it speaks both to my intelligence *and* my emotions. Their flights are, on average, probably $300-1000 more expensive than standard commercial flights ... and worth it to me. Why? Because they challenge the status quo and answer the question nobody thinks to ask: "Why do we have to keep doing things the way we've always done them?"

If you guessed from reading this that I value innovation, problem-solving, creativity, and outside-the-box thinking ... you're correct. That's what a brand is - the visual, verbal, and emotional expression of a set of values reflected in business. That's why we respond viscerally to specific brands and ignore others.

When I (Jason) started the ThinkerGrowth community, it took a little while to come to life. One reason for the delay was that I needed to get the right people on the bus; I'd started too many ventures alone. I'm determined to travel the remainder of my journey in a community with like-minded people. I've "been there, done that" chasing dollars and success for its own sake.

It was only when those right people emerged that our Tuesday workshops and community offerings began to flow freely. The same will happen for you. Whatever you treasure but fail to acknowledge or integrate into your brand will, ironically, deprive you of customers you could have otherwise. Creating a brand that accurately reflects you is the kindest, most appealing thing you can do for your potential customers.

We've assembled some questions about your brand for you to answer. How you answer them will tell you how closely you've paid attention to this critical step. You can bypass it if you want, but beware—many businesses fail in part because they skip it.

Can you name your organization's values, vision, and mission and explain how they benefit your target customers?

For Emissary, we adopted the tagline, "Helping faith-driven founders and entrepreneurs tell the stories that matter." In those eleven words, the target customer gets a clear picture of what we're up to, and so does everyone else. You can read a statement like that and safely assume a few things:

- Our brand means "a collaboration with experts," as opposed to a stenography service
- It's aimed at people who have some degree of religious faith
- There are stories that "matter" versus ones that don't matter

If you follow through to the point of interacting with us, your experience will be consistent with the tagline. We reject 99 percent of the people who inquire about working with us, usually because they're not "ready" to become successful, published authors who tell stories that matter.

Does your brand's visual identity trigger the emotions and associations you want to evoke from your audience?

Visual identity is essential to your brand. In subtle and subconscious ways, it communicates how well you understand your values–and, therefore, how attentive you are to your audience's preferences and expectations. Everything from colors and fonts to your willingness to engage visual learners and consumers factors into a successful brand.

But those are the basics. Colors, fonts, and videos only carry you so far. For visual identity to connect on an emotional and subconscious level with a prospect, your brand needs to speak very clearly toward solving the audience's problems *the way they perceive or feel them.*

Several years ago, I (Jason) worked with a client who owned a lawn care business in my hometown. I looked over his website and found a vast array of snafus.

The first problem? The photography. Believe it or not, he used photos taken with his digital camera of lawns belonging to his real-life clients. Authentic as they were, the images would give potential buyers the opposite of what they wanted to feel. Looking at the pictures, I thought, "I could pay my son ten bucks to do this."

The second problem was verbal. This was back in the early 2010s when marketers overemphasized search engine optimization (SEO). While there's nothing inherently wrong with SEO, it gets messy when copywriters pay zero attention to the context and placement of keywords. One sentence even included the exact keywords "in Rockford" at the beginning and the end of the sentence.

The bottom line was that my client's website was "too busy," with jargon everywhere. It was like viewing a lovely home filled with clutter from one end to the other.

We reworked his website to include stock and professional photos of beautifully manicured lawns, deleted significant amounts of copy, and replaced them with a simple phrase that projected competence to match the images: "We service over 1 million square feet of lawns every week." Then, we set up a small estimating tool for potential clients to enter the approximate size of their lawns and instantly calculate their projected price.

My client never looked back, and his business grew slowly.

Is your brand voice consistent throughout your marketing activities?

Until the time of writing, Bud Light was the preeminent beer brand for traditional, heterosexual American men who love to watch and discuss sports in their spare time. Though they faced stiff competition from competitors like Coors and Miller, no brand was more prevalent or closely aligned with professional sports leagues like the National Football League than Bud Light.

Bud Light's voice sent a clear message, over and again, to this target demographic: "We're like you. We cut loose on the weekends, crack jokes, open a 'cold one,' and enjoy the game on the weekend."

Anheuser-Busch underestimated the fallout of their decision to embrace identity politics and partner with a transgendered activist as a new spokesperson. National sales dipped by more than 25 percent, and to date, they have not recovered; Bud Light's most loyal customers took their business elsewhere. The brand's voice had changed; they made clear that they took their primary customer base for granted.

Your brand has a voice. Call it what you will—a "vibe," a "feeling," an emotional wavelength. When people interact with your brand, they subconsciously associate it, using terms like *fun, serious, offbeat, aspirational, future-oriented,* etc.

Bud Light's changed tone caused a ripple effect. There was the apparent departure from their traditional messaging, but also a profound, subconscious shift – from the tone of a casual weekend buddy who drops by to watch the game to a religious lecturer demanding a massive change in personal values from their buying audience. The irony of an alcohol producer presuming to lecture customers on morality and social responsibility fell as flat as their 'Please drink responsibly' warning labels – only this time, it pushed customers away.

Does your brand's personality reflect your values and resonate with your audience?

The Ford Motor Company caters to the upscale segment of its audience through the Lincoln brand of cars and SUVs.

In recent years, they've leveraged the personality and voice of actor Matthew McConaughey, who appears casual, relaxed ... and yet thoughtful and reflective, dressed in business casual clothes, driving his Lincoln MKZ, often at nighttime and gazing at city lights, processing his thoughts out loud. His musings are both meaningful and humorous, subtly poking fun at himself without sacrificing serious thought.

Who do you suppose Lincoln wants to reflect through this personality? Someone who thinks freely and independently? Someone who lives an affluent lifestyle and appreciates nuance? Perhaps someone full of ambition and desire yet wise and experienced enough to know their limitations? Someone who hopes to be noticed by the opposite sex like McConaughey would if he drove Lincoln through town?

If "brand voice" reflects the tone and demeanor of your brand, *personality* might correspond to how it interacts with others – word choice, style of dress, social context, and affiliation. For example, the Super Bowl is famous for its advertising rates, and the commercials take on a life of their own during the game. However, certain brands don't participate; you never see commercials from luxury names like Dolce & Gabbana and Louis Vitton during the Super Bowl because the event is inconsistent with their brand personalities.

As you build your brand, it's wise to consider its personality. If your brand came to life as a human being, how would he/she show up? How would they dress? Who would they hang around? Which other brands would be their "best buddies"?

Does your brand consistently reflect your values, visual identity, voice, and personality?

I (Paul) perceive Jason's "Thinker" brand the way I perceive the man himself–I might use the phrase "quirky, eccentric brilliance" to describe him. That essence shows up across the spectrum of his brand.

From our earliest conversations, I detected a high level of self-sufficiency in Jason. He didn't "need" my help when he agreed to hire me to coach him through writing his first book. He could have done it himself. He chose to hire me because he'd transcended his independence, which is not easy to do.

Yet despite his commanding demeanor and tremendous inner reserve of competence and intellectual aptitude, Jason retains a quirky sense of humor, which causes the "red airplane" logo and his "Coffee With Humans" podcast to align with his brand. His bottomless appetite for understanding how to harmonize technology, communications, and strategy shows up in every conversation with each other and author candidates.

Brand consistency goes deeper than matching colors and dialogue. It results from detailed, intimate awareness of your identity, strengths and weaknesses, wisdom, and experience. It channels through aligned and refined outlets to a carefully selected audience with whom it will likely resonate.

Bonus tip: A shortcut to creating a consumer brand is modeling the style based on a movie your customer would like. This works well for franchises and restaurants that "theme" the experience, from carpet to decorations to tableware, around scenery from popular films. Down home cookin' from Machine Shed (a Midwestern staple) speaks differently than the Italian atmosphere of Olive Garden. But in both cases, to set foot in these locations is to enter a particular environment, which gets reinforced from one end to the other.

Hopefully, this chapter helped you see the thought and energy that go into building your brand. In the next chapter, we'll look closer at choosing your channels.

Chapter Four
Pro Bono Publicity

What if you want to connect with someone who has no interest or is too busy for networking groups? We certainly do. Faith-driven founders, executives, and entrepreneurs make their fair share of appearances—but not with the general public. They're also challenging to reach via the channels they display on their websites; cold e-mail and phone calls usually find their way to junk folders, gatekeepers, and personal assistants.

During my (Paul) days as an insurance agent, several people advised me to build relationships with real estate agents. It sounded good - but realtors are habitual appointment cancelers. There's an 85% chance they'll reschedule. If a client wants to see a home, they drop everything and run, notifying you with a text on the way.

So I thought, "If I can't nail them down for lunch and they're always on the go, where do they get 'pinned down' somewhere I can casually interact with them?"

An idea came to mind: *open houses*. Realtors publicize them ahead of time and spend the entire day there, showing people around. Much of that time gets spent tapping on a keyboard, waiting for someone to appear.

You don't want to interrupt a realtor's day or distract them with idle chit-chat. The last thing you want is to put them in the tricky spot of asking you to leave. You need a compelling reason to go to an open house—long enough to create a connection and short enough to avoid being a nuisance.

Luckily, there was a good reason for me to be there - I was building my Facebook following. I wanted to make meaningful content, so I switched hats and behaved like a publicist, bringing a one-man film crew to create accessible content on the realtor's behalf.

I recorded and narrated video tours of their listings, briefly interviewed the realtors, uploaded the videos to Facebook, and shared them with my audience.

Now, to a realtor who is putting time, energy, and money into marketing a property, do you think my presence *enhanced* their open houses or detracted from them?

Welcome to the world of Pro Bono Publicity.

The wonderful thing about our modern time is that anyone and everyone with a smartphone can act like a publicist. All businesses need help with marketing and awareness. Jason says, "An average product that's well-marketed is better than an excellent product nobody knows about."

If you want to create inroads with a business owner ... help them promote their business by showing genuine curiosity.

There are plenty of ways to do this, even if Facebook doesn't fit with your current work. The media world is **democratized**—you no longer need to work at a PR firm to help people tell their stories. You just need to be curious about them and help them gain exposure using whatever channel works best for you.

Choosing the Channel

I (Jason) built a following on TikTok. I enjoy the format, and the content resonates with the audience. During winters in the Chicago metro area, I'll walk in the snow and share my thoughts and wisdom. When I wrote my first book, *What Could Be*, I derived principles and lessons from interactions with my TikTok audience.

If you delve into sharing and promoting others' businesses, I suggest you begin with a channel where attention is plentiful. Paul and I use LinkedIn to market Emissary, for example, but not in the same way I use TikTok for my brand. LinkedIn has nothing like the "stickiness" of TikTok ... we create content on LinkedIn, but we don't expect much from it.

The point is this: you may not need a channel where people get mesmerized by video content. You may only need a venue suitable for searching for people and connecting with them individually through private messages. Many business owners do just fine using Facebook and LinkedIn that way – we certainly do! So, think about the appropriate channel ahead of time. The last thing you want to do is start a channel that requires you to spend enormous amounts of time and energy creating content ... when a simple personal outreach will do just fine.

Identify the Audience

Some channels are stronger with specific demographics than others. LinkedIn caters to middle-aged business owners and professionals, while Instagram and TikTok are popular with younger generations. Chronologically, most entrepreneurs struggling to build their businesses and lives are likely to be younger than me, and the lion's share of attention from young people shifted to TikTok during the pandemic ... so that's where I planted my feet.

If you've identified the audience that aligns with your brand, you should know where to start sharing your message. The first element for a successful recipe is finding a medium where people pay lots of attention; the second is determining where *your* niche audience fits.

The third (and most important) part is to soberly assess the credibility you can "command" from your audience. As a trained speaker with hundreds of live workshops and teachings, I'm very comfortable doing "personal musings" videos on TikTok. I have abundant experience and stories to draw on and can articulate their moral lessons easily. If you're not quite as comfortable talking about what you know, "talking head" videos might not suit you.

Consider your Goals

If you sell small, inexpensive products or low-ticket content like courses, it's worth asking whether you can turn channels like social media, podcasts, or your e-mail list into profit centers.

On the other hand, if you're selling high-ticket items, like professional services or real estate, you're likelier to be in the game of building awareness, brand recognition, and a marketing funnel.

Each category requires a different approach, but the former is usually *transactional* (buy now), while the latter is more *relational* (education, infotainment). So, if you're selling high-ticket consulting services, focus on messaging that steers people into a relationship with you versus messaging that steers them toward making a purchase.

As publishers, we get to do a mixture of this. Books are low-ticket, low-barrier-to-entry commodities almost anyone can buy. So, we can easily market a $25 message to a wide variety of readers who fit the description of our authors' target readers.

On the other hand, we can also use the occasion to share the books we publish with our target clients because there's usually some overlap. Our books concentrate on personal, professional, and spiritual development ... and so do our prospects. It makes it easy to build trust and relationships with them.

Evaluate the Channels

TikTok is an emotional medium, as is most video content, and I (Jason) want to reach people through connection. Simple videos in my studio generate some traffic, but the "walk in the snow" videos give the viewer a sensory experience.

On the other hand, TikTok is not an excellent place to hold audiences' attention for extended periods through a single piece of content. Our various offerings, such as webinars and the *What Works* and *Emissary Authors* podcasts, are more suitable for that crowd. "Binge" audiences are more interested in details and background and prefer to get "swept up" in your educational material.

Consider your channel's merits and weaknesses, particularly if you plan to do paid advertising at some point. You might have to work through a channel different than the one you prefer simply because it caters to the right audience.

Test and Refine

A friend of ours in the videography business shared his commitment to posting regular, quality content. That's the precursor to testing and refining. If you skip this step, good luck—you'll end up doing a whole lot of guesswork. If you're going to test and refine, you'll need more than a single piece of content or the occasional email.

An old saying goes that "sales is a numbers game," and so is marketing. Publish consistently, and you'll either get a response or you won't. If you don't get a response after a steady stream of sharing, you can recalibrate and try something / somewhere else. What didn't work in the first quarter on LinkedIn may work well on Twitter / X in Q2.

Metrics are the simplest way to tell whether people care about your message enough to give it time out of their day. Remember the four categories of your audience? You can expect champions and supporters to open your emails or listen to your podcast episodes. But resistors and bystanders need more coaxing ... which means you probably have some work to do if your metrics "flatline" at a certain level.

Quality Over Quantity

Don't spread yourself across *every* platform or channel until you've gained traction in one or two. You'll get burned out and exhausted, and content creation will consume your life. It's better to produce quality content for a single channel.

I (Paul) have always done well on Facebook, mainly when being humorous in print. I share jokes, one-liners, or "theater of the mind" posts that stir my audience to create mental pictures. It's a personality quirk, but it works in tandem with giving people a window into my life and how I think.

But I don't do any of that when I post on LinkedIn and YouTube. The audiences there could be less interested. I ditched Instagram, TikTok, and Twitter to focus on audiences of business professionals and personal friends.

It takes time to find out what channel works best for each person. So commit yourself to consistent outreach via 1-2 channels until you get a signal.

Duplicating Your Presence

One day, after I (Paul) had networked and used Facebook nonstop for several months, a woman who'd recently started a business in Olympia approached and asked me to spill my secrets.

"I don't understand how you can be in 10 or more networking groups per week," she said, incredulous. "I can't find the time to go to all those groups, and still take care of clients and run my business."

I paused for a moment, to be sure that I understood her correctly. I knew one thing for sure: I never attended 10+ networking groups per week.

"What do you mean?" I asked.

"Well," she continued, "I've gone to about a dozen different groups. In every single one of them, someone at the meeting asked me, 'Have you met Paul Edwards? He's a member of our group!' All of them said you were a member of their group! How do you find time to do that?"

It suddenly dawned on me: even though I was not *technically* a member in 10 out of 12 of the groups she mentioned ... I had succeeded in creating the perception that I was.

The beauty of Pro Bono Publicity is that "what goes around, comes around." Once you put yourself out there, promoting others and their businesses, those people tend to reciprocate – often, without awareness that they're doing it. They talk about you (pleasantly and positively) behind your back, even when you're not in the room or affiliated with the circles they belong to.

So don't hold back on becoming a pro bono publicist for your network, because it will transform them into your unpaid sales force.

In the next chapter, we'll look closer at how you can harness the digital world to create your own version of being seen everywhere.

Chapter Five
The Profitable World of Nonprofits

During my insurance days, I (Paul) joined the local subchapter of the Association of the US Army (AUSA). We supported soldiers and families stationed at Joint Base Lewis-McChord, Washington. I joined and participated with expectancy; I knew that simply showing up and offering what I had would spark our trusty friends - magnetism and reciprocity.

Then, I joined the Miss Thurston and Miss Lewis County (Miss America) pageants, where I served as a mock judge and emcee. Nonprofits have a way of sparking organic conversations. Camaraderie occurs without effort through shared work projects. Trust accelerates. And where there are conversations, camaraderie, and trust, sales are sure to follow.

I noticed an irony about nonprofits – 90 percent of the volunteers and donors were entrepreneurs or business development/salespeople. Hardly anyone who participated did so out of pure, unadulterated altruism. Nobody ever said, "No thanks, I'm just a volunteer," if you expressed interest in doing business with them. So while I agree – nonprofits are not the place to become "salesy," the fact remains that everybody who participates in one gets *something* ... because healthy human interaction *always* implies exchange.

I am not interested in the ethical debate between for-profit and nonprofit companies.

Nonprofits get their money from *somewhere*. They don't print it, like the government. It doesn't grow on trees. Nonprofits get money from *donations*—from people who own businesses and work jobs, who have disposable income, usually by working in the for-profit sector. I respect the nonprofit industry and have spent much time volunteering in it. But without the private sector, it's as defunct as any for-profit business. Cash flow is cash flow, no matter your tax status.

So one day, I quipped to myself, "Not-for-profit IS for profit," and the saying stuck. The main difference is how the tax man looks at them, and who cares what the IRS thinks?

One Nonprofit, Profiting Another

As planning began for the 2016 Miss Thurston pageant, the board members said they wanted to find local "celebrity" judges—prominent community leaders whose names or brands were recognizable to the audience. I suggested John Setterstrom, CEO of the Lucky Eagle Casino in south Thurston County. Everyone thought it was a good idea ... but how could we contact him?

"Leave that to me," I told them. "I'll track him down."

The next day, I had lunch with my friend Cameron Wilson, a real estate agent who told me he planned to attend a fundraiser for the 2016 candidate for governor of Washington.

As we talked about it, he mentioned several people he expected to attend, including ... John Setterstrom.

"Do you know him?" I asked.

"No," Cameron replied, "but I know he will be there. I'll add you to the guest list."

Bingo. I had my chance to meet John.

In the interim, I met with the board of AUSA, who wanted me to create a new fundraiser based on my monthly "Cigar / Poker Night" event. Suddenly, the cards all fell into place ... maybe we could get a deal by holding it at the Lucky Eagle Casino!

"I think I know how to make this work," I told the board. "I'll report back when I have more."

I went to the political fundraiser, and Cameron introduced me to John. Handing him my business card, I said, "I'm glad I got to meet you because I'm on the board for the Miss Thurston County pageant, and we're looking for celebrity judges, and your name came up."

John's face broke into a wide smile. "That sounds fun!" he said, returning his card. "Send me an e-mail. I *will* respond."

Two weeks later, I emailed to connect him with the pageant judges' chair. "By the way," I added, "I'm also on the board for AUSA, and we're looking to host a cigar/

poker fundraiser for soldiers and families. Do you think the casino would be willing to provide the space?"

A day went by, and then he wrote back, "Absolutely. I've cc'd my events manager, LuWana Hawley, and she'll get you set up."

I now had a judge for the pageant and a venue for a bunch of business guys to smoke cigars, play cards, and raise money for troops. The only thing that could have made it better was a new insurance client.

AND I Got a New Client

Did you think the story was over?

I went to the casino to discuss the cigar/poker fundraiser details. We met with LuWana, who saw my business card and said, "I've been looking for an insurance agent because I'm starting my own business!"

So now I'd procured a judge for one event and a venue for the other AND gained a new client.

The pageant went off like a hoot; the AUSA event raised over $4000, and LuWana became a longstanding insurance client.

So, should you become part of a local nonprofit? You have everything to gain and nothing to lose. Serving in a nonprofit shows leadership and commitment. You meet great people who are generous with their time and skill. You fulfill the Golden Rule, which is a crucial reason to be in business in the first place. You distinguish yourself, which is critical (especially if you work in a red ocean industry like insurance).

Keep this up long enough, and you'll be surprised when, sitting in your office making fundraising calls, RFPs and sales opportunities seem to "flow" to you through no effort of your own.

If They Tell You About Their Cause ...

Don't forget, as I shared in the example from the last chapter - if people in your network have causes they care about and promote, it's an automatic "inroad" for you to support them and build magnetism and reciprocity.

Once, a friend who coordinated marketing for my sons' private Christian school asked me to help procure items for their fundraising auction. I couldn't "donate" an insurance policy ... so I had to develop a better idea.

I knew two young ladies who networked in the area for Dell Computers. I asked them if they could donate a tablet as an auction prize, which they did. I also offered to introduce them to Talia Hastie, the marketing coordinator, and set up the introduction via email.

Several weeks later, Talia approached me excitedly to thank me for introducing the two young ladies from Dell. She told me that they'd met, and she'd learned about a particular educational discount program Dell created for private schools.

The school had plans to buy a bunch of new computers ... but now, thanks to Dell, they'd lopped $10,000 off their original allocated budget. I'd saved the school $10k and helped my friends at Dell procure more new business—all through one little email.

Another time, one of my clients joined the steering committee for her kids' youth sports club. They decided to put on a fundraising auction, and she approached me during a networking group for any support I could offer.

Standing next to us were some mutual friends in the massage business. I said, "Obviously, I can't 'donate' insurance ... but do you think people would bid on a couples' massage if I paid for it upfront?"

In my direct and peripheral vision lines, I saw all three heads nod rapidly in agreement, and I wrote a check on the spot. I used that strategy *many* times after that, and it always brought me goodwill and greater revenue.

There are too many good things to leverage by supporting and participating in nonprofits for you to stay in your office making cold calls. In turn and in time, what goes around comes around. As Proverbs says, "The generous man will himself be refreshed."

Chapter Six
The Content Game

In the last two decades, cross-border flows of data have leapt ahead of goods and services as the most heavily traded exports and imports. Human beings now earn more money from the exchange of information than they ever will from raw materials, manufactured goods, or services.

At the time of writing, the U.S. economy wrestles with both an ongoing labor shortage *and* a low unemployment rate. How can this be? One answer lies in what we just shared: human beings no longer need to search for jobs when they can sustain themselves through content creation.

Welcome to a wave of change similar to the one ushered in for our ancestors by the Industrial Revolution. They learned to go from working on farms and in fields to working in factories; we're learning to go from the traditional 9-to-5 to building personal media platforms (PMPs).

I (Jason) prefer to remain out of sight unless specifically approached and asked for my thoughts and opinions. I once took one of those "Spirit Animal" quizzes that identified me as a "falcon" – a reclusive creature that only emerges from its den to hunt prey. But when a falcon spreads its wings, it has a 100% success rate of finding its latest meal.

I host two podcasts, *Coffee With Humans* and *What Works*. Most of the guests I interview on those two shows get booked because they request it; I rarely take time to search for people actively, and I despise the work of coordinating schedules.

But if you want to hear people say, "I see you everywhere," it's 100 times more likely to happen if you actively publish content online and maintain an outbound schedule of appearances. Whether it's blogs, social media, videos, podcasts, or anything else – as an old saying goes, "Those who do, do ... and those who don't, don't."

When Paul and I decided to start the Emissary Authors Podcast, he led the charge on booking guests. What a relief for me! It left me free to work on the strategy behind our episodes, which we thought it would be helpful to share with you. This is how it works:

Identify audience pain points and interests

It's hard to know if your content will be helpful unless the audience is already interested. Fortunately, technology makes it simple to search for what's "trending" or "heavily searched" online. Before launching our show, we spent time researching and studying what people searched for online when they looked for ghostwriters and publishers.

We've made a point of interviewing authors who've already "been there, done that." They can speak authoritatively about what it truly takes to become a successful, influential, published author. From the get-go, one of our brand promises is to give people the straight-up, sometimes hard-hitting *truth* about being an author versus selling just the "sizzle." And the data is clear from the research—that's what prospective authors truly want to hear, too.

Choose the right format

As we build our audience for the podcast, we've released YouTube and audio-only versions to test whether we get a stronger signal with video versus without it. Some people convey things well on camera, while others "have faces for radio."

Also, pay attention to how you share your content on social media; if you use Twitter/X, the accompanying text for your post should be short and punchy. Some podcasts make their episodes 10 minutes long at most, while others go on for hours. We usually go for 30-40 minutes. In a world with a significant shortage of attention span, we recommend you default for shorter copy length and brief running times.

Later, you can let loose a little more when your audience is built and engaged. The best time to talk at length is when you already have a dedicated group of followers who will listen and provide ample feedback.

Craft a Compelling Headline

At the core of every interview we do is a crucial facet of being an author. Here are some of the titles we've created to drive that point home:

- "The Book I Never Wanted to Write"

- "Stop Wasting Your Time"
- "Tell the Whole Story"
- "The Real Reason You Write"
- "What It Takes to Get It Done"

Let's face it – you have only a few seconds to "hook" someone into consuming your content. You may as well give them a reason to raise an eyebrow and mutter, "Hmm ... this looks interesting. Let's see what this is about."

Create Valuable Content

But how do you define "valuable"?

This goes back to what you want to achieve in the first place. If you want people tuning in, subscribing, and regularly enjoying your content, sharing it with people they know and giving you feedback ... then you must make content valuable *to your audience.*

We often ask our authors, "What is 'for me,' and what is 'for thee'?" It's a quick rhetorical way of getting authors to think through what they're writing about. The object of persuasive communication is to find the "common denominators" in the topics we discuss – things that resonate with both the hosts and the audience. Your individual story is unique – but in the context of spreading a message, it's like a vehicle for connecting with the audience. Once you have their attention, you turn to what you have in common with them.

So if you're going to share information that is usually reserved "for me," make sure you can apply it to the everyday, unchanging, irreversible realities of human existence ("for thee").

Be Consistent

If you show up 48 out of 52 weeks a year, everyone has a scheduling conflict now and then. Your audience and network may not even notice your absence because they're so accustomed to your presence. If they do, they'll easily forgive/excuse it. Everyone has to skip a standing engagement now and then.

However, if you show up only four weeks out of 52, don't be surprised that you remain unheard of. One of the fanciful illusions of the internet marketing age is that, with the clicks of a few buttons and a couple of homemade videos, you, too, can be a multi-millionaire.

Contrary to widespread assumption, the people who hawk their services online invest *years, decades,* and *dollars* to reach the level of brand awareness and offers they lay before you in their content. They're nothing if they're not <u>consistent</u>. Some of them show up every single day in your email inbox. Their video content never stops flowing. Their podcast episodes number in the thousands.

One word about this, however – ubiquity can also go too far. One of the quickest ways to discredit yourself is to "talk for the sake of talking." Many content creators today invest time into planning a "content calendar," where they pre-select topics for discussion each week. It's exhausting (not to mention cringe-worthy) to force yourself to drone on. If you can't think of anything to discuss … sometimes, keeping your mouth shut is better.

The Subject That Must Not Be Named

When I (Paul) began using Facebook to build my brand, I received wise counsel from a mentor: "Don't talk about insurance. No one wants to hear it, and no one cares. Instead, talk about your passions, interests, family, hobbies, sense of humor – *anything* but insurance."

I took his advice to heart. The only time I brought up insurance was when I parodied myself as an insurance salesman, such as with memes featuring Ned Ryerson, the smarmy sales caricature in *Groundhog Day*. The rest of my content centered around personal interests, water cooler conversations (such as football "pick 'em" threads), photos of my family, funny videos, and so forth. Eventually, people who were relative strangers reached out for help with insurance and said, "I feel as though I know you, even though we've never met." Bingo.

Of course, if you're marketing a product or service everyone enjoys talking about, feel free to disregard my advice. Just beware, however, that even with the coolest gadgets or luxury services, people still purchase from brands they *connect* with. Connection occurs both in the conscious and subconscious regions of the mind, and usually happens when one person detects similarities and "echoes" of themselves in another.

That's a fancy way of saying, "People buy from people they know, like and trust."

In the next chapter, we will share strategies for building the "KLT" factor, even with high-profile people who wouldn't normally give you the time of day.

Chapter Seven
Networking with Dream Connections

I (Paul) was in my late twenties when I first read *Wild At Heart*, John Eldredge's *New York Times* bestseller that awakened a generation of Christian men. It was the first time in a long time I felt someone go bone marrow-deep on my faith. I read through the entire book in one sitting, in one night – and then I reread it, and reread it again.

At that moment in history, it was safe to assume the only way I could ever meet John was by attending a *Wild At Heart* "Boot Camp" in the mountains of Colorado or one of his speaking engagements. Even if I could somehow get in front of him, there was no way I'd get to have more than a brief conversation. I'd met enough prominent people to believe the best I could get was an autograph and a handshake.

A decade went by. I spent several years hanging on John's every word in his books. I never thought I'd get to meet him or talk at length with him. It was painful because I regarded him as a more excellent mentor than anyone I could find in my local church. I loved how he explained the Gospel and the profound respect his writing showed for the depth of the average person. He was one of the few Christian authors I'd encountered who made me feel "seen, heard, and understood" without knowing who I was.

To make a long story short, events and the arc of my life conspired to bring me to *Wild At Heart* Boot Camp in 2017.

Focus on the Farm Team

I didn't get to talk to John while I was there, but I <u>did</u> meet one of the key leaders of Wild At Heart - Morgan Snyder, who'd started a spinoff podcast and retreat called *Become Good Soil*. We enjoyed a brief conversation where I told him how much I appreciated what he shared on the show ... and then I went on with the life-changing weekend.

There are many ways to network with a "dream connection," but by far, I think the most important thing you can do is **engage the people in their inner circle** —the people who have influence on the prominent person you want to meet. So be quick to make friends with the "farm team."

About a year after the retreat, I started my podcast, *Influencer Networking Secrets*. As I researched possible guests, I wondered if Morgan would be willing to give an interview. He'd recently published an episode about relational styles - which I found inspiring and illuminating. So I wrote to him, mentioning that I was a Boot Camp alum, and asked if he'd be willing to appear on my show to share what he'd learned. He agreed.

The following spring, I noticed another voice on the *Wild At Heart* podcast - Allen Arnold. In those days, he was promoting a book he'd written called *The Story of With*, and I wanted to discuss his background in the publishing industry. So we scheduled an interview built around the "hero's journey" literary style and talked for nearly an extra hour after we finished recording.

At the end, I asked Allen if John had any new books in the works and whether he thought John would be willing to appear on my show when it came time to promote his next one.

Allen replied that John was working on a new book called *Get Your Life Back*, which was due to be published in February 2020. He told me that if I contacted John's publicist and mentioned that I'd interviewed Allen and Morgan, there was a good chance I could book my longtime mentor as a guest.

In February, John joined *Influencer Networking Secrets*, which I broadcast over Facebook Live. It was an interview for the ages - I was finally face-to-face in a private, lengthy conversation with one of my greatest heroes and mentors.

Building quality, genuine relationships with the people who surround a prominent leader ... creates opportunities.

Be An Angler

If you've ever watched an expert fly fisherman, you'll know that they catch their fish by simulating an insect flying over the water. The bait on the end of their line might be real ... but it's not flying alone. Unfortunately, the fish below the water can't tell the difference.

When you go to a public setting to meet people, you look like everyone else. There's no way to distinguish yourself until you open your mouth and speak. By opening their mouths, most people reveal that they hope to transact business.

You must show, by what you say, that you're there for *business reasons.* "Business reasons" means you're there to open or enhance relationships; "transact business" means closing sales and making money.

Neither of these is invalid in context; you might be a *vendor* at an event. In that case, it's fine to close sales and make money. But for networking with Dream Connections, it's unseemly.

So go for business reasons – if you think back to my story of meeting John Setterstrom to recruit him as a pageant judge, that's an example of a business reason.

Keep Your Ear to the Ground

Dream Connections have little idea of what's available or doable in their spare time. They usually have an entourage or team that keeps them busy around the clock. The last thing they want to hear from you is one more business opportunity or responsibility they must manage or show up for.

But can you create an easy path for them to relax, have fun, and let loose? Now, *that* is a different approach.

I once did this for Andy Ryder, the mayor of Lacey, Washington. Andy is a firearms enthusiast, and he wanted to try out Glacier Gun Club, a local indoor firing range in downtown Olympia. You could fire rounds and shoot targets, and they even had a ventilated cigar lounge in the back where you could sit, smoke cigars, and talk business. I'd recently become a member there.

I set up an afternoon of relieving stress, popping off rounds, smoking cigars, and talking business one-on-one. I brought him in on a guest pass, bought a bunch of ammo, and brought my own cigars, cutters, and drinks. All Andy had to do was show up, walk in, sign waivers, and start enjoying himself.

Who does things like *that* for people like him? You can count them on the fingers of one hand.

I believe you should *never* approach a Dream Connection with something that adds more weight to their calendar. Instead, create a space for them to unplug and unwind from the pace and demands of their day-to-day life.

Done-For-You Publicity

As a publisher, this next piece is part of my daily routine. I learned to do it long before I was in the publishing business.

Some of what we've covered in the "Pro Bono Publicity" chapter applies to this list I borrowed from my friend, John Corcoran. You can help a Dream Connection by:

- Recording or writing a review of their product/service
- "Buying" some of their time

- Ask for an interview
- Attend their conferences, speaking engagements, or special events
- Reach out with a heartfelt, handwritten note
- Honor them with an award

One thing I've learned about Dream Connections is that the higher you climb the success ladder, the less the dollar figures matter. They become preoccupied with *impact* - "Is my message resonating? Am I having an impact on people's lives? Is all of this worth my while?" As my friend Kevin Thompson says, "Revenue is a byproduct of making an impact."

It's wise to understand this "dialect" of Dream Connections. If they are preoccupied with impact and significance, you should be, too.

Equally important - the more you speak the language of people who perform at that level, the likelier you are to be *elevated* to that level - which is an excellent place to be if you want to attract clients or customers based on your *reputation* rather than how many hours you put into making sales.

Chapter Eight
Leadership

Leadership came naturally to me as a young man in multiple professional scenarios. In my early twenties, I excelled in telephone customer service positions, partially because I took "ownership" of each call, showed up early, stayed late, and worked overtime when it was offered.

To become a leader, the first person you learn to lead is *yourself* - and I demonstrated in those jobs that I prioritized my employer's success over leisure time, self-indulgence, and my feelings at the moment.

Similarly, my superiors in the Army promoted me quickly to noncommissioned officer status because I demonstrated robust self-regulation. They never had to tell me to shine my boots, shave my face, show up on time, or what uniform to wear. That, together with combat experience, was enough to be regarded as mature and capable of wielding authority.

An Old War Story

During my first deployment to Iraq in the summer of 2004, I languished for nearly six months, doing 8-16 hours a day of guard duty, often at night. I regretted that I'd signed up and come all this way just to stand in a guard tower. My fellow soldiers worked daylight hours on the resupply mission. That was where my platoon's "action" was - but I never got to do it.

My superiors had good reason to exclude me. They couldn't count on me to do our vehicles' basic, routine maintenance tasks. I'd botched an early mission by failing to secure food items in the truck I drove, spilling them into the streets for local Iraqi kids to swoop in and pick up. As far as my superiors were concerned, I belonged on guard duty - unless I could prove my reliability to them.

One night, I fell asleep in the guard tower and got caught. They punished me. Legally, they could have gone further and demoted me, cut my pay, and required me to do extra duty, but they stopped short of that punishment.

But I was *ticked*, and I decided, "Somehow, I have to get off guard duty."

I approached the platoon leadership with a written rotation schedule to give everyone in the platoon a break from guard duty and showed it to them.

The idea surprised them. They didn't agree to the entire plan but were willing to give me a shot personally. They said, "If you can show us that you're responsible every day, you can be on the Log-Pac mission."

That was all I needed. From that day until we left, I never pulled another shift of guard duty. I took <u>ownership</u> of my responsibilities. I did the daily maintenance drills, refueled the vehicle, swept it, rolled up cargo straps, cleaned the windows, checked the fluids, and cleaned my rifle.

As a reward, I got to participate in some memorable missions - including nighttime missions delivering ballots and election materials to local voting precincts. Iraq held its first free elections since 1979, and *I got to be part of them*. It's among my most treasured memories as a soldier - and it all started with showing <u>leadership</u>.

In most social settings, there are opportunities to distinguish yourself from the crowd. You simply need to make the shift from a "tenant" mindset (showing up to see what you can *get*) to an "owner" mindset (showing up to see how you can *give*).

Proximity Equals Power

During my insurance days, a friend encouraged me to give a presentation on networking. He saw that I was calm and engaging as a speaker to groups. So I began to do a 15-minute talk called "Networking Intentionally." Whenever I gave it, people walked up afterward to give glowing feedback, and several asked for reviews of their insurance programs.

Today, I belong to an online mastermind group. Over 150 faith-driven businessmen are members, and the leadership approached me about hosting "New Member Orientation Calls."

I accepted without hesitation because I remembered the power of leadership with my local networks. Whether I emceed pageants, organized poker games, or sat on the board of the chamber of commerce, people automatically viewed me as authoritative. They'd look to me for answers to questions, or introductions.

I don't serve in leadership because it puts money in my pocket. Instead, it's about meeting new people, listening to their stories, helping them get acclimated, and (most importantly) connecting them with other people they should meet.

My main currency is *trust*, more than money. What's the use of having money that belongs to people who don't trust you? How long do you think you'll get to keep it?

Two Types of Leadership

There are two types of leadership: **positional** and **influential**.

Sometimes, showing leadership means you carry an official title; other times, you just have to be the person others look to when they need guidance, information, or introductions. Leaders express themselves best through *action*.

When I escaped guard duty in Iraq, there was no promotion or increase in pay. I simply took ownership of my role on the resupply mission ... and it drastically changed things, so the second half of my deployment was a *lot* more impactful, memorable, and aligned with my hopes and expectations.

So forget about titles and let your leadership skills show through your actions. You'll reap plenty of benefits for your business. To succeed in networking and business development, <u>volunteer in a leadership role</u>.

Conclusion

We hope these lessons and examples steer you clear of wasted time, money, and energy - and into the promised land of building a brand strong enough to prompt others to say, "I see you everywhere!"

If you are a faith-driven business owner or developer looking to build and market a personal brand, particularly through the written word, you may be interested in learning more about Emissary Publishing.

You can go to our website, PublishWithEmissary.com, if you want to learn more.

And we'd love to hear your stories about implementing what we teach in this book. Feel free to look us up on social media:

LinkedIn: https://linkedin.com/company/emissary-publishing

Jason: https://www.linkedin.com/in/jasonatodd/

Paul: https://linkedin.com/in/meetpauledwards

*Scan for more
stand-out ideas!*

Emissary Weekly Digest

✕ **Fluff**

✓ **Marketing tips**

✓ **Book recommendations**

✓ **Podcast recommendations**

✓ **... and even more goodness!**

About The Authors

<u>Paul Edwards</u> is the co-founder/publisher, chief executive officer, and editor-in-chief at Emissary Publishing in Phoenix, Arizona.

Paul is a Spanish-speaking US immigrant, a two-time Operation Iraqi Freedom veteran, and a devoted student of Ancient Jewish Wisdom. He is a 3X published author and has ghostwritten ten books and over 2 million words per year.

A disciple of the Messiah, Jesus of Nazareth, Paul enjoys bodybuilding, copious amounts of sunshine outdoors, and spending time with his bride, Shannon, and their two sons, Grant and Chase.

<u>Jason Todd</u> is the co-founder/publisher, chief operating officer, and marketing strategist at Emissary Publishing's Chicago office.

Before joining Emissary, Jason founded, grew, sold, and exited five businesses over two decades. He wrote over 1 million lines of code, transitioned into advising hundreds of organizations and teams, created brand identities for small- and medium-sized businesses, produced hundreds of audio/video creative episodes, and managed negotiations with billion-dollar companies.

A resident of Rockford, Illinois, Jason enjoys hiking, rock climbing, playing music, singing, and spending time with his family.

Emissary
PUBLISHING

Emissary tells the stories that matter.

When you publish with Emissary, you get the amount and kind of support you need - from start to finish, and everything in between.

	Emissary	Hybrid	Traditional
Author Strategy	✓	✗	✗
Personal Brand Development	✓	✗	✗
Ghostwriting	✓	✗	✗
Professional Editing	✓	✗	✗
Publishing Logistics	✓	✓	✓
100% Author Creative Control	✓	✓	✗
No Minimum Author Purchases	✓	✗	✗
Fixed Royalties (no percentages)	✓	✗	✗
Fulfillment (Print & Ship)	✓	✗	✓
Book Launch Press Outreach	✓	✗	✓
Pitch Articles (online, print)	✓	✗	✓
Webinar & Livestream Management	✓	✗	✗
Book Signing Events	✓	✗	✓
Podcast Interviews	✓	✗	✗

Learn more at PublishWithEmissary.com